Our Age

Jack Bemporad and
Michael Shevack

Our Age

The Historic New Era
of Christian-Jewish
Understanding

Foreword
by
John Cardinal O'Connor

New City Press

Published in the United States by New City Press
202 Cardinal Rd., Hyde Park, NY 12538
©1996 Jack Bemporad and Michael Shevack

Cover design by Nick Cianfarani

Library of Congress Cataloging-in-Publication Data:

Bemporad, Jack.
     Our age : the historic new era of Christian-Jewish understanding /
Jack Bemporad and Michael Shevack ; foreword by John Cardinal
O'Connor.
          p.   cm.
     Includes bibliographical references.
     ISBN 1-56548-081-3 (pbk.)
     1. Judaism—Relations—Catholic Church.   2. Catholic Church—
Relations—Judaism.   3. Judaism—Relations—Christianity—1945–
4. Christianity and other religions—Judaism—1945–   I. Shevack,
Michael.   II. Title.
BM535b.B377   1996
296.3'872—dc20   96-25774
                                                                              CIP

Printed in the United States of America

Contents

To
Russ and Angelica Berrie,
whose vision for a world of religious harmony,
and whose efforts to achieve it,
have been a source of personal inspiration
to us both.

And to Rose Abrams,
who lived what true religion is all about.

Foreword

Some prospective readers may never get beyond the Introduction to *Our Age*. They will bristle over what they will perceive as a "pack of lies," a vicious assault on Christianity, a grossly one-sided account of Jewish sufferings at the hands of Christians. The more will be the pity, if such occurs. They will be depriving themselves of as honest and evenhanded a treatment of Jewish-Christian relations as I have ever read, and I have shelves filled with carefully studied literature on the subject.

The Introduction reveals the seeds of hatred sowed centuries before Hitler, seeds that by his day had flowered into a culture that made the Nazi abominations possible. Does this introductory treatment of centuries of tragedy present the entirety of the story, nuanced to the satisfaction of every historian or interpreter of the events recounted? I suspect that the authors would be the first to reject such an hypothesis. They are synthesizing in a handful of pages nearly two thousand years of relationships. In my judgment, sadly, the thrust of their synthesis, painful as it is to Christians, is unerringly on the mark and provides crucial context for the chapters that follow. These chapters concern themselves eloquently with the shocking Vatican II document, *Nostra Aetate* (Our Age) and ensuing events.

To call *Nostra Aetate* less than "shocking," I would suggest, would be to betray significant naivete, or even denial, about how bad relations between Jews and Christians in general had been for so many centuries. As *Our Age* observes, one Jewish leader called the document a "turning point"; a Catholic leader, a "daring presentation."

How *Nostra Aetate* has been received, the struggle to make it known, the efforts on both sides to integrate it into both international and daily personal relations, such questions are addressed with nothing less than exquisite fairness. As a Catholic who for many years has attempted to contribute, if ever so fractionally, to the advance of Jewish-Christian understanding, I find myself proud of what the Church has been doing in the years since *Nostra Aetate* to compensate for past injustices, to heal today's breach and to offer hope for the future. That Pope John Paul II has taken giant steps to lead the entire Church in this regard must be without question; nor do the authors question it. On the contrary, their praise breathes through the entire text.

Jewish leaders have not been idle, nor have they refused to take risks. By both their honest criticism and their sympathetic understanding, they have made dialogue a joy and mutual respect a mutual habit.

Our Age will help both Jewish and Catholic leaders immeasurably in efforts already undertaken together. Of at least equal importance, it offers every responsible reader an opportunity for new insights into the extraordinary dynamic of reconciliation between and among brothers and sisters, children of the same Father.

I am deeply grateful for *Our Age*.

John Cardinal O'Connor
Archbishop of New York

Introduction

This is for those who dare to believe. For those who dare to believe that the past need not condemn the future, that enmity can be transformed into trust, that good can be chosen over evil.

This is for those who dare to believe what all too often seems hard to believe: that people can change.

There are wonderful signs of change. Walls within nations have been torn down. Cold wars are giving way to warmer alliances. Iron curtains have been drawn open. Maps are being re-drawn with kinder boundaries.

For many, these changes seem to have sprung up suddenly, just within a few years of our most recent decade. Yet, way back in 1965, perhaps the first, most fundamental, and in many ways, the most miraculous of these world-shattering changes took place. The Roman Catholic Church, reflecting deeply upon her own inner consciousness, took bold courageous steps to put an end to one of the most ancient of all human scourges: anti-semitism.[1]

Jew. Christian. For nearly twenty centuries, virtually all of the "Christian era," they have remained separate and antagonistic. For nearly twenty centuries Jews have suffered unspeakable horrors, as they attempted to survive the brutal prejudices of misguided people, who professed themselves Christian in name, but not in deed.

This, however, was not always the case. The earliest Christians *were* Jews. Jesus' apostles were Jews. Mary was a Jew. And, though many Christians often do not stop to realize it, the very cornerstone of the Christian faith, Jesus of Nazareth, was a Jew.

Early "Christianity" was a movement within Judaism. "Christians" still honored the traditions of the Jewish Fathers. They kept kosher, followed circumcision, obeyed the Torah, and upheld the authority of the sages. They differed only in the belief that Jesus was the Messiah, and that his return, along with the final redemption of the world, was imminent.

With Saul of Tarsus, Saint Paul, a separation began to take place between Jews and followers of Christ. Paul carried the belief in Jesus' messianic mission outside the confines of ancient Judea, spreading it throughout the world, which was at that time culturally Greco-Roman.

Paul differed significantly in his viewpoint from other apostles. He felt that it was not necessary for Gentiles to circumcise themselves, or obey the many other laws of Judaism in order to become "Christians." They need only *believe* in Jesus as the Messiah, accept him "in faith." Needless to say, in a culture where Jewish customs often seemed alien, burdensome, and in the case of circumcision, painful, Paul's belief held a powerful attraction.

If the distinction between Jews and Christians had not been very clear up till now, it soon became so. Greek-Roman Gentiles became the more numerous source of converts to the new Jewish movement.

The culture of the ancient world had been well-seeded for this event. In fact, well before Paul, many Gentiles had already begun to believe in One God; they had begun to believe in "monotheism," as the Jews taught it. They had become aware of these ideas in discussions with Jews who openly sought converts.

These Gentiles who accepted the God of Israel were described as "God-fearers." They did not follow all the customs of Jews; they remained uncircumcized; and yet they believed in the very same God. It was with this population that Paul's preaching had special meaning. For now they could be not merely "God-fearers," but could begin to fully participate in a true *covenantal* relationship with God. They too could be "adopted" into the historic mission to morally transform the world, which began with the Jews.

The relationship between Jews and early Christians continued, but with increasing resentment. Jews increasingly saw Christians not as a Jewish sect, but as heretics. Christians came to see Jews as turning their back on God's revelation. Christianity began to develop its own independent theology, which contained ideas, such as the incarnation, which were considerably different from traditional Jewish thought, and in many respects seemed contrary.

The pivotal transition point in the separation of Jews and Christians came during the time of Hadrian. Pagan Roman persecution had the effect of pitting Jews and Christians against each other. And so, the divergence of the two religions took place; two faiths, two brothers born from the same root, went two separate ways.

During the fourth century, there was a dramatic change in the character of Christianity. Emperor Constantine embraced Christianity and made it the official religion of the Roman Empire. During this same period, every attempt was made to sever any lingering relationship between Judaism and Christianity.

The Jews became perceived as "enemies of Christ," barriers to the one true faith, which for Rome was Christianity. Judaism was viewed as a primitive stage in the evolution of Christianity. It became touted as an antiquated "religion of law," as opposed to the Christian "religion of faith." Jews were seen as "infidels" — literally "without faith." The Jewish refusal to accept Jesus as the Messiah became seen as an act of treason against Christendom, turning them into enemies of the state.

Moreover, by resorting to scripture, many Christians blamed Jews for the crucifixion itself. And over the years, this would become the theological justification for untold cruelty and inhumanity.

With the dispersion of the Jewish people, residing more and more in Christian territories, they were subjected to more and more religious and political persecution. During the Middle Ages, Jews were forced to debate the truth of their beliefs in a Christian "kangaroo court"; these notorious *Disputationes*, which the beleaguered Jewish community could never win, became justification for still more persecution. Jews were tortured, massacred, burned at the stake. The Inquisition in Spain murdered countless Jews because they refused to accept forcible baptism.

Vicious rumors spread throughout Europe that Jews used the blood of Christian children in making Passover matzohs, the so-called "blood-libel." Even the bubonic plague, which decimated the population of Europe, was blamed on Jews poisoning the wells. These absurd superstitions became yet more justification for persecution.

Many Popes condemned these charges, and there were many kind, sincere, and honorable Christians who were appalled by this behavior, many Catholic clergy who refused to participate in the persecution of Jews and even helped rescue them. But the fact remains that anti-semitism spread like a cancer throughout Christian society.

For close to eighteen centuries, Jews suffered beyond imagination at the hands of professed Christians. The memory of this persecution is so ingrained in the minds of Jewish people, that even today just the word "Christian" can feel like a threat to Jews, a threat both to their faith and to their lives. The cross, a symbol for Christians of grace and reconciliation, is, for many Jews, a symbol of persecution and violence.

A certain improvement began to take place with the advent of democratic ideas after the Age of Enlightenment. But the old prejudices were not easily relinquished. No matter how Jews tried to integrate into society, they were still considered outcasts, a threat to the government and "good Christian" citizens. Economic woes and political problems were all blamed on the Jews.

This sorrowful state of events did not stop at modern times, for in the twentieth century the most vicious, most incomprehensible form of anti-semitism emerged: the Nazi Holocaust. Hitler's plan to eradicate this ancient God-chosen people almost succeeded. Mass incarceration, mass extermination, mass biological experimentation lead to the eradication of six million Jews — virtually the entire Jewish population of Europe.

In addition to Jews, three million Poles, most of whom were Catholic, lost their lives, as well as millions of gypsies, Serbs and Slavs.

The Nazis were not Christians in any sense of the word. They were pagans: worshiping only themselves and their own brutal power. Their plan was to wipe God off the planet, and they began with the first people to recognize God: the Jews. The Nazis began their attack on Western civilization with an attack on the most ancient religious institution in Europe: the synagogue.

But, on the surface, the Nazis *appeared* to look like ordinary Christians. Indeed, many Nazis came from Christian families, some attended Church, and it is undeniable that virtually all came from a Christian culture, which had for too long tolerated anti-semitism. It is of little doubt to either Christian or Jewish scholars that early Christian theology and the long history of Jewish persecution contributed to the anti-semitic nature of the Holocaust.

It was this belief that lead a Jew, Jules Isaac, a French professor of history, to radically awaken the

Christian conscience. Himself a severe sufferer under Nazism, surviving the death of many family members including his wife, Isaac made it his sacred mission to study Christian scripture and the theology of the Church Fathers to demonstrate, once and for all, the relationship between early Christian theology and anti-semitism. His conclusion was summed up in the title of his important book: *The Teaching of Contempt* — for this was, he claimed, what Christianity had done.

Isaac's work soon caught the attention of well-intentioned Christian scholars and theologians around the world, and especially that of a kindly old man: Pope John XXIII.

An extraordinary humanitarian with immeasurable love and warmth, John XXIII had a vision. He called it, in Italian, *aggiornamento,* a "bringing up to date." And so he initiated the remarkable Church self-transformation and modernization we now refer to as "Vatican II."

It was the most systematic, most thorough and most dramatic change in the Church the world had ever seen. It was a total re-statement, and in very many instances, a purification of the ancient Church's teachings, to harmonize them with the spirit of democracy and freedom which was spreading throughout the world. Forsaking religious prejudice for religious respect, Vatican II threw open the doors of the Church to embrace all religions as containing truths of God. Consequently, a new spirit of openness emerged, fusing itself into the body of the Church.

16

However, of all the changes Vatican II brought, there was one that would literally change the world; it would take the entire current of historical events leading up to the Holocaust and single-handedly, decisively, reverse them. It was the tiny section 4 in the Vatican II "Declaration on the Relationship of the Church to Non-Christian Religions," which heralded a new era: "our age," the meaning of its opening Latin words, *nostra aetate.*

These few paragraphs were the culmination of all of Jules Isaac's work. They were the fulfillment of a promise made to him in a meeting with Pope John XXIII.

Nostra Aetate was the seed of a whole new relationship with the Jews. The beginning of the end of Catholic anti-semitism. The beginning of the end of theologically-justified anti-semitism. The beginning of the end of the notoriously, inhuman suffering which Jews had often experienced at the hands of Christians, who should have behaved as "brothers and sisters."

The theological prejudice which had plagued the Jews for many years had been addressed. The roots of the Holocaust were severed.

Over the years, the seed *Nostra Aetate* had planted would begin to bear fruit, transforming the relationship of Jews and Catholics permanently.

Soon other documents emerged, dealing with the relationship between Jews and Catholics in ever-increasing detail. The *Guidelines* in 1974 and the *Notes* in 1985 all expounded and expanded the "good news" that *Nostra Aetate* had brought. Soon there emerged a solid body of Church teachings that made the return to anti-semitism literally impossible: *Anti-semitism had been declared anti-Christian.*

Greater miracles were soon to happen.

In 1986, the world Jewish community witnessed an unprecedented event: the first visit by a pope to a synagogue. At the synagogue in Rome, John Paul II declared the Jews to be Christians' "elder brothers." The Pope personally set a living example for all the Catholic faithful to follow.

But perhaps the most startling and most human event of all occurred at a conference in Prague in 1990. The then Archbishop, now Cardinal Edward Cassidy, speaking for the Church, openly and publicly asked forgiveness from the Jewish people for all the suffering the Church had inflicted upon them.

This was soon followed by the heroic efforts on the part of the Church to stop a new wave of anti-semitism which, after the collapse of the Soviet Union, had begun to re-emerge in Eastern Europe. In 1991 a "Polish Bishop's Statement" was read aloud in every church and parish in Poland a sign to the world that the Church would no longer tolerate anti-semitism from her faithful.

This was followed in 1992, by the publication of a new world catechism which sought to eradicate anti-semitism through the power of education.

And last but not least, in 1993, through the initiative of John Paul II, the Holy See established full diplomatic relations with the modern State of Israel.

As earthshaking and history-shaking as these events are, ironically, and sadly, hardly anyone knows about them.

Far too many Christians go about their daily lives harboring the same old prejudices their Church has forsaken. Far too many Jews go about their daily lives with no "sigh of relief," unaware of these remarkable new Catholic teachings.

The time has come to make all these things known, to bring these extraordinary events and teachings to every Jew and Catholic in the world. That is our purpose here.

The process of Jewish-Catholic reconciliation is not easy. There are many difficult roads ahead, many unresolved issues, issues far too complex to mention here. They are difficult for most theologians, let alone lay people. So we have endeavored to keep things simple, to present clearly and concisely the new teachings of the Roman Catholic Church, and what they mean to both Catholics and Jews, but in a way everyone can understand.

Moreover, we have done everything possible to condense the long history of suffering and persecution within this introduction. This should never be interpreted as a desire to give it short shrift or to broom it under history's rug and forget it. It is simply a desire to concentrate on the miracles taking place today.

Painful memories take time to heal. Prejudiced hearts don't easily love. No one can quickly erase the consequences of such a bitter history. Nevertheless, we need to begin.

In the few decades since Vatican II, more has been done to change the relationship between Jews and Christians than in the preceding twenty centuries. Hopefully, it will not take quite as many generations for the changes to take place where ultimately they must: in the human heart.

And so, we challenge you:

Whether Christian or Jew, we dare you to confront your own prejudices. We dare you to believe, truly believe, that people can change. And that the world can be a better place for all God's children.

After twenty centuries, Judaism and Catholicism have embraced as brothers. Cannot individual Jews and Catholics do the same?

This is the promise of *Nostra Aetate*. This is the promise of *Our Age*.

Opening Doors

One Jewish leader called it a "turning point," "a new beginning destined to overcome centuries of misunderstanding, enmity and even hatred and persecution."[1] A Catholic leader, called it "an absolute unicum . . . never before had a systematic, positive, comprehensive, careful and daring presentation of Jews and Judaism been made in the Church by a Pope or a Council."[2]

What they are referring to is section 4 of the "Declaration of the Relationship of the Church to Non-Christian Religions," which by Catholic and Jewish scholars is now simply referred to as *Nostra Aetate*. *Nostra Aetate* was the seed from which grew all the miraculous events to follow, the beginning of a new world for Jews and Catholics.

But to enter this new world is impossible without a deeper understanding of the vision, the dream behind Vatican II.

That dream was simple but profound: After centuries of religious divisiveness and political hostilities, the Church had made the decision to lead the world to a new vision of the future; a future of peace, of mutual understanding, of love for, and of love among, all God's children, regardless of race, nationality or religion. That dream was begun by Pope John XXIII; but, step by step, it was transformed into reality by his successors Paul VI, and then John Paul II.

This was not merely a dream, but a necessity. The world had changed considerably since 1869, the year Pius IX convened the First Vatican Council. After two world wars, Western governments now openly embraced the spirit of democracy, with its rights to freedom of conscience and religion. "Human rights" had become the focus of the Western political agenda. Moreover, the scientific age had now become a part of everyday life. Science and technology had opened up new possibilities for freeing the world from the ancient scourges of starvation, poverty, and disease. Advances in communication and transportation took a world, which once seemed all too large, and made it seem much smaller. The economies of the world's nations had become increasingly dependent upon each other; the livelihood of someone in one part of the world was affected by the livelihood of someone in another part. The biblical ideal of "one humankind" seemed to be becoming an historical fact, as it continues to become today.

Therefore, the mission of the Second Vatican Council could not be to merely address the Catholic faithful. Vatican II needed to reach out to Catholics and non-Catholics alike, to all peoples, all religions, all cultures and faiths within the one humankind. This mission can be seen and felt throughout all the Vatican II documents, but especially in "The Dogmatic Constitution of the Church," known by its opening Latin words, *Lumen Gentium.* For many, this document was not merely a light but a beacon, the masterpiece of Vatican II, the first complete statement of Church doctrine by an ecumenical council in Christian history.

Of all the remarkable declarations in *Lumen Gentium,* the one which is of special significance here can be found in Chapter II, "The People of God." Heralding a new age of understanding and tolerance, *Lumen Gentium* stated categorically that all God's children, whether Catholic or non-Catholic, may receive God's salvation:

> Those who, through no fault of their own, do not know the gospel of Christ or his Church, but who nevertheless seek God with a sincere heart and, moved by grace, try in their actions to do his will as they know it through the dictates of their conscience, those too may achieve eternal salvation. Nor does divine Providence deny the help necessary for salvation to those who, without blame on their part, have not yet arrived at an explicit knowledge of God, but who strive to live a good life, thanks to his grace. (II, 16)

By clearly throwing open the door to the possibility of salvation for all humankind in *Lumen Gentium,* the Church now had a basis upon which she could establish loving relationships with members of every faith. She could fully appreciate the grace God had granted them through the truth contained in their different religions. Thus, the interreligious spirit of the age fused itself into the body of Church law. It was upon this foundation that the Church would create *Nostra Aetate*, throwing open doors to religious dialogue between Catholics and Hindus, Moslems, and all non-Christians, including Jews.

However, the relationship between the Church and the Jews is not at all like that between the Church and other non-Christians. It is a unique, special and complex relationship.

The Church views her mission, her very religious life, as an "adoption" into the covenant of Israel, and an "extension" of it. Through Abraham, God had established a covenant with the People of Israel, by which the redemption of the world would begin. This covenant blossomed under Moses and the prophets. Jesus as the Christ is for the Church the culmination of that covenant and the fulfillment of it. So in a very real sense, the Church has a kind of "inner Judaism." Deep inside her she has a relationship with the Jewish people as the "root" from which Christianity arose and draws strength. Jewish truths are at the very foundation of Christian truths, and indeed are inseparable from them.

Complicating the relationship between the Church and Judaism even more, is the fact that they do not agree on the identity of Jesus of Nazareth as the Messiah. Nor does Judaism agree with the Church's understanding of the *nature* of the Messiah as God's Lamb, whose blood was necessary for the redemption from sin.

From its onset, any statement about Jews and Judaism that the Second Vatican Council could make, had to walk a very delicate line. It needed to uphold the utmost respect for the Jewish people, without whom Jesus and Christianity would never have been born. It needed to acknowledge its debt to Jews and those Jewish truths that are at the foundation of God's covenant. But, at the same time, it was necessary to make clear the Church's difference of opinion, and her own unique interpretation of the meaning of Israel's history.

Therefore, the first accomplishment of *Nostra Aetate* was to strengthen the spiritual connection of the Church to the people of God's covenant, whom she refers to in *Nostra Aetate* as "Abraham's stock," emphasizing our common biblical heritage. In so doing, *Nostra Aetate* makes a clean break from the hatred, the persecution, and the anti-semitism of the past.

In *Nostra Aetate* we see a breakthrough — the first doctrinal statement in history that goes hand-in-hand with a warm, respectful, loving presentation of Jews and Judaism. It is so powerful, so dramatic, that we shall quote it in its entirety here:

> As this sacred Synod searches into the mystery of the Church, it recalls the spiritual bond linking the people of the New Covenant with Abraham's stock.
>
> For the Church of Christ acknowledges that, according to the mystery of God's saving design, the beginning of her faith and her election are already found among the patriarchs, Moses, and the prophets. She professes that all who believe in Christ, Abraham's sons

according to faith (cf. Gal 3:7), are included in the same patriarch's call, and likewise that the salvation of the Church was mystically foreshadowed by the Chosen People's exodus from the land of bondage.

The Church, therefore, cannot forget that she received the revelation of the Old Testament through the people with whom God in his inexpressible mercy deigned to establish the ancient covenant. Nor can she forget that she draws sustenance from the root of that good olive tree onto which have been grafted the wild olive branches of the Gentiles (cf. Rom 11:17-24). Indeed, the Church believes that by his cross Christ, our peace, reconciled Jew and Gentile, making them both one in himself (cf. Eph 2:14-16).

Also, the Church ever keeps in mind the words of the Apostle about his kinsmen, "who have the adoption as sons, and the glory and the covenant and the legislation and the worship and the promise; who have the fathers, and from whom is Christ according to the flesh" (Rom 9:4-5), the son of the Virgin Mary. The Church recalls too that from the Jewish people sprang the apostles, her foundation stones and pillars, as well as most of the early disciples who proclaimed Christ to the world.

As holy scripture testifies, Jerusalem did not recognize the time of her visitation (cf. Lk

19:44), nor did the Jews in large number accept the gospel; indeed, not a few opposed the spreading of it (cf. Rom 11:28). Nevertheless, according to the Apostle, the Jews still remain most dear to God because of their fathers, for he does not repent of the gifts he makes nor of the calls he issues (cf. Rom 11:28-29). In company with the prophets and the same Apostle, the Church awaits that day, known to God alone, on which all peoples will address the Lord in a single voice and "serve him with one accord" (Zep 3:9; cf. Is 66:23; Ps 65:4; Rom 11:11-32).

In these first few paragraphs, the Church expresses the "spiritual bond" which links her to Abraham's people. Stressing the teaching of Paul, himself a Jew, the Church emphasizes that she "draws" the spiritual "sustenance" for her mission from Jewish "roots"; indeed without these roots there would be no Church. That the word "draws" is in the present tense should not be overlooked; with it, the Church is emphasizing the continual spiritual importance of Jews, even to this day. Jews today continue to "have [that is, in the present] the adoption as sons, and the glory and the covenant and the legislation and the worship and the promise." God's "promise" to the Jewish people, God's covenantal gift to them, their "adoption" as the Chosen People, the "glory" of their law, has not been diminished or been invalidated after Christianity.

Quite to the contrary, Jews continue to represent the living, breathing promise from God which, as the Letter to the Romans expresses, is eternal: "God's gifts and his call are irrevocable" (11:29). If many Christians in the past considered Judaism a fossil from an earlier stage in the evolution of Christianity, this is not the Church's current position.

Thus, *Nostra Aetate* opened a door to true Christian theological respect for the irrevocable Jewish covenant, a major theme that shall be strengthened and re-strengthened over the years. Now that this is firmly in place, the Church urges Jews and Catholics to open up a deep, meaningful dialogue, including religious and theological discussions:

> Since the spiritual patrimony common to Christians and Jews is thus so great, this sacred Synod wishes to foster and recommend *that mutual understanding and respect* which is the fruit above all of biblical and theological studies and of brotherly dialogues. [emphasis added]

As we have already mentioned, past religious discussions between the Church and Judaism were often bitter contests between faiths. But now the Church assures Jews that any theological discussions between them shall be "brotherly," conducted with the utmost understanding and respect on both sides.

This respect, which continues into the next paragraph, is for many, the climax of the entire statement:

True, authorities of the Jews and those who followed their lead pressed for the death of Christ (cf. Jn 19:6); still, what happened in his passion cannot be blamed upon all the Jews then living, without distinction, nor upon the Jews of today. Although the Church is the new people of God, the Jews should not be presented as repudiated or cursed by God, as if such views followed from the holy scriptures. All should take pains, then, lest in catechetical instruction and in the preaching of God's Word they teach anything out of harmony with the truth of the gospel and the spirit of Christ.

For those Jews who have grown up being called "Christ killers" by their "Christian" neighbors, *Nostra Aetate* now banishes this horrible accusation, once and for all. Jews are not "repudiated or cursed by God"; no passage from scripture should be used to portray them as such. It bears repeating, Christ's "passion," that is, his crucifixion, "cannot be blamed upon all the Jews then living, without distinction, nor upon the Jews of today."

This is not to say that there were not some Jewish authorities, especially under pressure from Roman authorities, who may have urged Jesus' death. However, be this as it may, this fact should not be used to justify persecution against all Jews and all Jewish authorities, either today or existing at that time:

29

The Church repudiates all persecutions against any man. Moreover, mindful of her common patrimony with the Jews, and motivated by the gospel's spiritual love and by no political considerations, *she deplores the hatred, persecutions, and displays of anti-semitism directed against the Jews at any time and from any source.* [emphasis added]

Anti-semitism *"from any source,"* including the Church,[3] is a deplorable act of inhumanity and contrary to the spirit of the gospel.

Besides, as the Church has always held and continues to hold, Christ in his boundless love freely underwent his passion and death because of the sins of all men, so that all might attain salvation. It is, therefore, the duty of the Church's preaching to proclaim the cross of Christ as the sign of God's all-embracing love and as the fountain from which every grace flows.

Since, according to Catholic doctrine, Jesus gave his life *freely* on the cross to redeem humankind, the discussion of "blame" for Jesus' death, makes little sense. Jew and Roman, apostle, relative, and friend, everyone surrounding the mystery of Jesus' crucifixion, were all participants in a drama which the Church believes was designed by God to inaugurate a new era of peace and love. Therefore, anything other than peaceful and loving relations between Catholics and Jews undermines the *very purpose* of God's own decree to sacrifice his Son.

Thus, through the doors opened by *Nostra Aetate*, the strong, penetrating light of our age entered, dispelling the shadows of the past, illuminating the hopes of tomorrow. But for millions of Jews and Catholics around the world it was just the beginning.

Nostra Aetate would mean a new life for both Jews and Catholics. A life fresh and invigorated by the open, generous, humanitarian spirit of the Second Vatican Council; a life freed from hatred and enmity; a life embracing the shared Jewish and Catholic love of the One God, Creator and Redeemer of all humankind.

History had been set on a new course.

The Dialogue Begins

Nostra Aetate had opened the door to the possibility of a relationship between Jews and Catholics. But it was up to the world Jewish community and the Church to walk through that door together.

In order to encourage that process, not very long after the end of the Second Vatican Council the Church created the Office for Catholic-Jewish relations. This was reciprocated in the world Jewish community by the merging of several major Jewish organizations to create a new one, the International Jewish Committee on Interreligious Consultations (IJCIC).

In December 1970 in Rome, the world was to witness another remarkable event: the first formal, respectful meeting between the Church and the Jews. At this historic meeting, a "Memorandum of Understanding" was created, which would serve as a foundation for the new relationship, and which outlined areas of common concern. It was also agreed to set up a permanent International Liaison Committee as a bridge between these two faiths.

In order to strengthen this organizational framework further, in October 1974, at the suggestion of the Liaison Committee, Pope Paul VI authorized setting up a special Commission for Religious Relations with the Jews. And just two months later, on December 1, 1974, this commision issued the next important document in Jewish-Catholic reconciliation, its "Guidelines and Suggestions for Implementing the Conciliar Declaration *Nostra Aetate* (no. 4)," now simply called the *Guidelines*.

As its name states, the purpose of the *Guidelines* was to implement *Nostra Aetate*. Such an implementation was necessary precisely because *Nostra Aetate* was *doctrine,* and therefore by nature "inner directed." Both Jews and Catholics felt a strong need to begin to bring these new teachings from the Church's inner consciousness into the outer world. And to do that would require handling many pragmatic issues.

Moreover, many of the teachings of *Nostra Aetate* did not seem clear to Jews, because they were contained within the compact style of Catholic doctrine. Many Jews felt the need to strengthen *Nostra Aetate* and translate it into more direct, everyday language.

For Catholics, the *Guidelines* would serve an additional purpose. It would begin to outline an approach, an attitude, a feeling that Catholics could take in opening dialogue with Jews. This was critical.

The *Guidelines* needed to create a new, more loving environment, a common ground upon which both Jews and Catholics could meet, one which would not threaten the truth of either faith. Indeed, there is much that Jews and Catholics have in common. After an expansive "Preamble," followed by a section dedicated to "Dialogue," the *Guidelines* highlights this in the area of "Liturgy," "Teaching and Education," and "Joint Social Action," before presenting its "Conclusion."

First, however, the *Guidelines* takes great pains to strengthen some of the weaknesses and to clear some of the ambiguities of *Nostra Aetate* from a Jewish perspective. If you remember, *Nostra Aetate* had merely *deplored* anti-semitism, and it did not mention the Holocaust. However in the *Guidelines*, the Church, finding herself "deeply affected by the memory of the persecution and massacre of Jews which took place in Europe just before and during the Second World War," *condemns* anti-semitism:

> . . . we may simply restate here that the spiritual bonds and historical links binding the Church to Judaism condemn (as opposed to the very spirit of Christianity) all forms of anti-semitism and discrimination, which in any case the dignity of the human person alone would suffice to condemn.

The "link" between Judaism and Christianity makes anti-semitism an affront to the Christian faith since, as the *Guidelines* reinforces, "Christianity sprang from Judaism, taking from it certain essential elements of its faith and divine cult." In short, to be anti-semitic is to be anti-Christian.

Our common heritage means that despite the "two thousand years, too often marked by mutual ignorance," Christians should now "strive to acquire a better knowledge of the basic components of the religious tradition of Judaism; they must strive to learn by *what essential traits the Jews define themselves in light of their own religious experiences.*" [emphasis added]

Because the Church believes Jesus to be the very same Messiah whom the Jews await, and because she believes Christianity to be the "New Covenant" which fulfills the "Old," oftentimes Christians have difficulty viewing Judaism as a living, flourishing, and independent faith with a God-ordained tradition of its own. In seeing Jews exclusively through the eyes of their faith, Christians, without intending to, can sometimes undermine the faith of the very Jews with whom they are attempting to establish a dialogue. Therefore, the *Guidelines* is careful to remind the faithful that:

> Dialogue demands respect for the other as he is; above all, respect for his faith and religious convictions.

This is not to say that in dialogue with Jews, Christians must cease to be Christian. Even though the Church no longer has an active mission to the Jews, Catholics still must, and always will need to, proclaim Christ Jesus as Lord. Nevertheless, the *Guidelines* cautions strongly against hurting Jews "even involuntarily," and recommends extreme "tact," as well as "a great openness of spirit":

> Lest the witness of Catholics to Jesus Christ should give offense to Jews, they must take care to live and spread their Christian faith

while maintaining the strictest respect for religious liberty in line with the teaching of the Second Vatican Council (Declaration *Dignitatis Humanae*).

These theological differences aside, there is much that Jews and Christians share that can serve as a firm foundation for dialogue between us. For both religions, "great causes such as the struggle for peace and justice" are all-consuming missions, which both Jews and Catholics could join in together. This kind of sharing could take place at the very depths of each of our religious identities, as we shall discuss in the conclusion.

The *Guidelines* also emphasizes the "links between the Christian liturgy and the Jewish liturgy":

> The idea of a living community in the service of God, and in the service of men for the love of God, such as it is realized in the liturgy, is just as characteristic of the Jewish liturgy as it is of the Christian one.

However, the greatest liturgical link between us is the Bible, which "holds an essential place" in both our traditions. For Christians this Bible includes both the so-called "New Testament" and the "Old." For Jews, this Bible includes only the "Old." This is often a source of friction between us, because these terms sometimes seem to imply that somehow the "Old Testament" is outdated, or antiquated.[1]

It is true that Christians differ in their interpretation of the Hebrew Bible,[2] especially in regard to messianic prophecy, considering the New Testament to have "fulfilled" or "completed" the "Old." However, this completion or fulfillment should never be construed to mean that the "Old" Testament has lived out its spiritual usefulness or importance. Quite to the contrary, the Hebrew Bible remains the Word of God to this day. It is that very same Word of God which Jews, with God's blessing, continue to revere. It is the very same Bible that Jesus, himself a Jew, based his teachings upon. The Hebrew Bible remains a never-ending source of wisdom and spiritual illumination that will always "retain its own perpetual value" (cf. *Dei Verbum* 14-15). Indeed, the very foundation of Christian scripture *is Jewish!*

That is why the *Guidelines* strongly cautions Christians not to set the "Old" Testament against the New Testament "in such a way that the former seems to constitute a religion of only justice, fear and legalism, with no appeal to the love of God and neighbor." In addition, the *Guidelines* cautions against distorting the meaning of Christian scripture, especially in those passages which "seem to show the Jewish people as such in an unfavorable light."

An example of this can be found in the Gospel of John, where we often see the expression "the Jews" seeming to condemn the entire Jewish people. In fact, this expression refers not to the entire Jewish people but to "the leaders of the Jews," or "the adversaries of Jesus." Another such example is the word "Pharisee" and "Pharisaism," which often seems to imply "hardened legalists" or "hypocrites." In reality, most of the Pharisees were pious, devout, God-loved Jewish scholars, the predecessors of the modern rabbi, to which Jesus had a special closeness, as we shall discuss in the next section. Indeed, "Jesus also used teaching methods similar to those employed by the rabbis of his time."

This is not to say that Jesus' teachings were identical to those of his Jewish contemporaries. "Judaism in the time of Christ and the apostles was a complex reality, embracing many different trends, many spiritual, religious, social and cultural values." The Church sees Jesus' gospel message as being of "a profoundly new character," differing in many ways from the opinions around him.

However, in many other respects Jesus does not differ at all from traditional Jewish ideas and teachings. In reading the New Testament, Jews often see Jesus reflecting the teachings of the great Jewish sage Hillel, who taught that "what is hateful to you do not do to your fellow human being."

All this only serves to highlight the shared spiritual history between us, and the link between Jews and Catholics, as *Nostra Aetate* defined it. Although for Christians, Jewish history is often understood exclusively in light of Christ and the gospel, this does not negate the fact that "the history of Judaism did not end with the destruction of the Temple." Judaism "went on to create a religious tradition," which faithful Christians adhering to Church teaching must respect.

In many essential ways we do not differ at all. After all, both Jews and Christians await "the day, known to God alone, on which all peoples will address the Lord in a single voice and 'serve him with one accord' (Zec 3:9)." For Christians, the word "Lord" means Jesus Christ, who is *fully God.* For Jews, the word "Lord" means simply God. How God shall ultimately resolve these different viewpoints in the course of modern history is once again part of the mystery of redemption.

In the meantime, though, it is important that both Jews and Catholics live together in harmony and love. To that goal, the *Guidelines* recommends a massive re-education program that includes revision of catechism, religious textbooks, history books, and the use of mass media such as newspaper, radio, cinema, and television. In addition, the Church recommends training instructors and educators in seminaries and universities as to the dynamics of the new Catholic-Jewish dialogue. It recommends, furthermore, substantial research into the remaining problems that exist between Judaism and Christianity, including the collaboration with Jewish scholars and even the creation of chairs of Jewish studies.[3]

Thus the *Guidelines* sets a foundation for the beginning of a true, loving dialogue between Jews and Catholics. And every day, this dialogue grows stronger. Hopefully it will one day be shared by the millions of Jews, and the over one billion Catholics around the world.

Deepening the Understanding

The wheels of change had been set in motion within both religious communities. Needless to say, there were a lot of questions — and the need to search for answers.

In March 1982, delegates of episcopal conferences and other experts met in Rome. Their mission was to create a guide that would be of use to all those in the Church who needed to present Jews and Judaism in line with the spirit of our age. Three years of preparatory work went into it. Several drafts were done. But ultimately the final version was released, entitled "Notes on the Correct Way to Present the Jews and Judaism in Preaching and Catechesis in the Roman Catholic Church," now simply called the *Notes*.

The *Notes* deals with many of the same subjects as the *Guidelines*, but the detail and depth make it an extraordinary achievement in its own right, as can be seen in each of its six sections.

In the first section, "Religious Teaching and Judaism," the Church emphasizes more strongly than ever before, the deep "spiritual bonds linking" Jews and Christians, and the "great spiritual patrimony" we both share through our ancient biblical heritage. It is a relationship which is "founded on the design of the God of the covenant," and therefore the Church has an obligation to emphasize the importance of Jews and Judaism in all her teachings. The Jewish presence in Church teaching "is essential and should be organically integrated."

Indeed, it is impossible for the Church to understand her mission, without understanding the Jewish people. As Pope John Paul II expressed it, "To assess it [Judaism] carefully in itself and with due awareness of the faith and religious life of the Jewish people as they are professed and practiced still today, can greatly help us to understand better certain aspects of the life of the Church."[1] Therefore, living Judaism is essential to the life of the Church; and the life of the Church cannot be properly understood without understanding living Judaism.

The *Notes* declares the relationship between Christianity and Judaism to be a "permanent reality." Using the words of John Paul II, the Jewish people are proclaimed "the people of God of the Old Covenant, *which has never been revoked.*" [emphasis added]

The eternal nature of the Jewish people, and the eternal relationship between Judaism and Christianity, reflect the "Relations between the Old and New Testament," the subject and title of the next section of the *Notes*.

For Christians, "the definitive meaning of the election of Israel does not become clear except in the light of the complete fulfillment (Rom 9:11)." Since, according to the Church, Jesus Christ is the promised Jewish Messiah, he is the fulfillment of Jewish prophecy.

This does not mean, however, that Judaism has been replaced or abandoned, and that the Jewish understanding of God is outdated. Quite to the contrary, understanding the vision of the Jewish people and their unique relationship with God, can help Christians to better understand the meaning of God's Word. The *Notes* recommends that Christians should try to see "the events of the Old Testament not as concerning only the Jews but also as touching us personally." Indeed, Christians should always remember that "the patriarchs, prophets and other personalities of the Old Testament have been venerated and always will be venerated as saints."

This is not intended to blur our separate identities. It is undeniable that Jews and Christians *are* different, that we *do* have different understandings about God. Nevertheless, the *Notes* carefully reminds us that "the people of God of the Old and the New Testaments are tending toward a like end in the future: the coming or return of the Messiah — even if they start from two different points of view. . . . Thus it can be said that Jews and Christians meet in a comparable hope, founded on the same promise made to Abraham (cf. Gn 12:1-3; Heb 6:13-18)."

None of us can know for sure every event, every act that God will take in the final drama of redemption. Therefore, it is important that the present differences in our points of view be respected as part of God's mystery:

> Attentive to the same God who has spoken, hanging on the same word, we have to witness to one same memory and one common hope

in him who is the master of history. We must also accept our responsibility to prepare the world for the coming of the Messiah by working together for social justice, respect for the rights of persons and nations, and for social and international reconciliation. To this we are driven, Jews and Christians, by the command to love our neighbor, by a common hope for the kingdom of God, and by the great heritage of the prophets.

This is a statement that all Jews and Christians can agree on.

In the next section of the *Notes*, "Jewish Roots of Christianity," the Church emphasizes even more strongly the Jewish roots of that olive branch onto which the Gentiles were grafted (Rom 11:17-18). The Church begins with an astounding fact of which very few modern Jews and Catholics are aware: "Jesus was and always remained a Jew; his ministry was deliberately limited 'to the lost sheep of the house of Israel' (Mt 15:24). Jesus is fully a man of his time, and of his environment — the Jewish Palestinian one of the first centuries, the anxieties and hopes of which he shared." Moreover,

There is no doubt that he [Jesus] wished to submit himself to the [Jewish] law (cf. Gal 4:4), that he was circumcised and presented in the Temple like any Jew of his time (cf. Lk 2:21, 22-14), that he was trained in the law's observance. He extolled respect for it (cf. Mt 5:17-20) and invited obedience to it (cf. Mt 8:4). The rhythm of his life was marked by observance of [Jewish] pilgrimages on great feasts, even from his infancy (cf. Lk 2:41-50; Jn 2:13; 7-10, etc.). The importance of the cycle of the Jewish feasts has been frequently underlined in the Gospel of John (cf. 2:13; 5:1; 7:2, 10, 37; 10:22; 12:1; 13:1; 18:28; 19:42, etc.).

It should also be noted that Jesus often taught in the synagogues (cf. Mt 4:23; 9:35; Lk 4:15-18; Jn 18:20, etc.) and in the Temple (cf. Jn 18:20, etc.), which he frequented, as did the disciples, even after the resurrection (cf., for example Acts 2:46; 3:1; 21:26, etc.).

Indeed, God chose the Jewish people and a Jewish family to bring Jesus into the world. Christians should not understand this to mean that Jesus was born *only* for Jews. The Church considers Jesus' birth and death as being a redemptive act for all humankind. Both "Jewish shepherds and pagan wise men are found at his crib (Lk 2:8-20; Mt 2:1-12)." And "at the foot of the cross there are Jews, among them Mary and John (Jn 19:25-27), and pagans like the centurion (Mk 15:39 and parallels)."

Though this is considerably different from the Jewish understanding of Jesus, it does not mean that Jesus and the Jewish sages at his time, also called the Pharisees, were totally at odds with each other.

Although careless interpretation of Christian scripture has tended to portray an image of the Pharisees as always being opposed to Christ, the *Notes* states that this is not the case. "It is Pharisees who warn Jesus of the risks he is running (Lk 13:31)." Jesus praises some Pharisees, such as "the scribe of Mark 12:34," and even "eats with them (Lk 7:36; 14:1)." Also, "Jesus shares, with the majority of Palestinian Jews of that time" some of the teaching of the Pharisees, such as "the resurrection of the body; forms of piety, like alms-giving, prayer, fasting (cf. Mt 6:18)," including the custom of praying to God as "Father," as well as "the commandment to love God and our neighbor (cf. Mk 12:28-34)."

Besides, even Paul himself "considered his membership of the Pharisees as a title of honor (cf. Acts 23:6; 26:5; Phil 3:5). Like Jesus himself, Paul also used methods of reading and interpreting scripture and of teaching his disciples which were common to the Pharisees of their time," including parables in Jesus' ministry, as well as "the method of Jesus and Paul of supporting a conclusion with the quotation from scripture."

It is also important to realize that the Pharisees, the predecessors of the rabbis, "are not mentioned in the accounts of the passion." There is no blame at all imputed to them. Quite to the contrary, Rabban Gamaliel, a famous rabbi, much-revered within the Jewish tradition, "defends the apostles in a meeting of the Sanhedrin (Acts 5:34-39)."

Therefore, the *Notes* states emphatically, "an exclusively negative picture of the Pharisees is likely to be inaccurate and unjust." And therefore, faithful Catholics should do everything possible to revise their understanding of these great Jewish scholars, the spiritual ancestors of today's Jewish rabbis. If, at times, the gospels seem to indicate "all sorts of unfavorable references to the Pharisees," it is important to understand that not all Pharisees were alike. Differences of scholarly opinion is something which has always been a part of Judaism, and Judaism at the time of Jesus was a very complex and diversified movement. If there were some Pharisees with whom Jesus appears especially severe, "it is because he is closer to them than to [any] other contemporary Jewish group." Theological debates among rabbis are very common in Judaism, and even in the rabbinic literature one can find criticisms of the various kinds of Pharisees. Therefore, in a very real sense, Jesus' disagreement with certain Pharisees could be seen as part of a rabbinical tradition which permitted different points of view.

In light of this, both Jews and Christians should be very careful in how they interpret scripture. Understanding the events, the people, the personalities, and the religious parties at the time of Jesus is a complex matter. This is emphasized by the next section of the *Notes*, "Jews in the New Testament," which quotes *Dei Verbum* 19:

> The sacred authors wrote the four gospels, selecting some things from the many which had been handed on by word of mouth or in

writing, reducing some of them to a synthesis, explicating some things in view of the situation of their Churches, and preserving the form of proclamation, but always in such fashion that they told us the honest truth about Jesus.

Therefore, as the *Notes* makes clear, it is entirely possible that "some references hostile or less than favorable to the Jews" are the result of conflicts between the newborn Church and the Jewish community. Indeed, certain controversies related in the New Testament may reflect Christian-Jewish relations long after the time of Jesus.

This does not throw into doubt the account of the gospels that "the majority of the Jewish people and its authorities did not believe in Jesus." This is most certainly the case, and remains the case to the present age. "There is no question of playing down or glossing over this rupture. To do so would only blur the separate religious identities of Jews and Catholics, to which God entitles them both."

Even so, the *Notes* adds, "there is no putting the Jews who knew Jesus and did not believe in him, or those who opposed the preaching of the apostles, on the same plane with Jews who came after or those of today. If the responsibility of the former remains a mystery hidden with God (cf. Rom 11:25), the latter are an entirely different situation."

This idea, in principle, should also be heeded by Jews. *The Catholics who once persecuted Jews are certainly not the Catholics of our age, and Jews should do everything possible to remind themselves of this.* It is important for us both to remember that "we should never judge the consciences of others." And although faithful Christians should pride themselves on the truth of their faith, this religious pride should never be allowed to become "proud"; as Paul in Romans 11:18 warned, "do not boast" in your attitude to "the root."

As the words of Vatican II's "Declaration on Religious Liberty"(#2) makes clear, "all men are to be immune from coercion . . . in such wise that in matters religious no one is to be forced to act in a manner contrary to his own beliefs. Nor . . . restrained from acting in accordance with his own beliefs."

In the next section of the *Notes*, "Liturgy," another "common ground" is established between Jews and Catholics. Though superficially Jewish and Catholic worship seem vastly different experiences, the fact is there are many similarities: "Jews and Christians find in the Bible the very substance of their liturgy: for the proclamation of God's Word, response to it, prayer of praise and intercession for the living and the dead, recourse to divine mercy." Many of the phrases used in Catholic worship are identical to those found in Judaism. Many of the prayers in Christianity sprang from Judaism just as the "New" Testament sprang from the "Old."

Perhaps the most remarkable of parallels can be found in the central prayer of the Christian faith, the Our Father, which Jesus himself had taught. Structurally, this prayer is undeniably Jewish, undeniably

Pharisaic, and very similar to the prayers still used today by Jews.

Besides the parallels between Jewish and Christian worship in terms of prayer, there are also considerable parallels in regard to religious holidays. For instance, Jews and Christians both celebrate the Passover. For Jews, this "historic Passover," which commemorates the Exodus from Egypt, also looks forward to the future arrival of the Messiah. For Christians, for whom the Messiah has already come, the Passover commemorates the faith-event by which the world was prepared for redemption: Jesus' death and resurrection. Therefore, for both Jews and Christians, the Passover is a holiday of liberation. It remains for both a " 'memorial' which comes . . . from the Jewish tradition."

Although faithful Christians consider Christ the culmination of Jewish history, this does not at all mean that Jewish history ended with the coming of Christ, as is discussed in the final section of the *Notes*, "Judaism and Christianity in History."

Even with the destruction of the great Temple of Jerusalem in 70 A.D., Jewish history went on. Judaism flourished in the rabbinical period, in the Middle Ages, just as it continues to do so in modern times. The dispersion of the Jews from the ancient land of Israel, what Jews call the *Diaspora,* repeatedly became a challenge of survival for the Jewish people. The *Diaspora* "allowed Israel to carry to the whole world a witness — often heroic — of its fidelity to the One God and to 'exalt him in the presence of all the living'

(Tb 13:4), while preserving the memory of the land of their forefathers at the heart of their hope."

In the year 1948 this hope was reborn with the founding of the modern state of Israel. The *Notes* states emphatically that Israel, like all legitimate nations, is deserving of strong, secure borders, according to "the common principles of international law."

The *Notes* sees the continued existence of the Jewish people as something ordained by God. Indeed, "the permanence of Israel (while so many ancient peoples have disappeared without trace) is a historic fact and a sign to be interpreted within God's design." It is a sign of the irrevocable covenant which God bequeathed to the Jewish people; it is living, historical proof of God's permanent relationship with the Jewish people as a witness for moral righteousness in the world.

For this reason, as the *Notes* concludes, repeating the words of *Nostra Aetate* and the *Guidelines*, the Church, "mindful of her common patrimony with the Jews and motivated by the gospel's spiritual love and by no political consideration, deplores the hatred, persecutions and displays of anti-semitism directed against the Jews at any time and from any source. . . . The spiritual bonds and historical links binding the Church to Judaism condemn (as opposed to the very spirit of Christianity) all forms of anti-semitism and discrimination, which in any case the dignity of the human person alone would suffice to condemn."

With the publication of the *Notes*, the process which began with *Nostra Aetate* and continued with the *Guidelines*, had reached a new depth of under-standing.

In just twenty years, a wound that had been open for centuries had finally begun to heal.

Elder Brothers

As much of a breakthrough as *Nostra Aetate*, the *Guidelines* and the *Notes* were, they were still documents. They were thought. They were word. They were part of a twenty-year process within the consciousness of the Church to affirm her faith in a way which also affirmed the eternal blessedness of the Jewish people. In this, they were an extraordinary success, setting a solid stage for the new relationship between Jews and Catholics.

However, once that stage was set, it was time for someone to step out on it. It was time to take these new words and thoughts and bring them outside the province of clergy and scholars. It was time for someone to take the lead and demonstrate to the entire world that our age had dawned, that the wound between Jews and Catholics could indeed heal. That person was none other than Pope John Paul II. If the great humanitarianism of John XXIII opened the doors of Vatican II, if the dutiful execution and elaboration of his dream was accomplished by his successor Paul VI, still, no other pope has said or done more to forge a spirit of love beween Jews and Catholics than John Paul II.

In Jewish communities all over the world, wherever this so-called "media Pope" has gone, he has stopped to preach the "new gospel" of Jewish-Catholic reconciliation — in England, Spain, Germany, Portugal,

Brazil, Australia, Austria, Italy, France, and of course, the United States, just to name a few:

> I am convinced, and I am happy to state it on this occasion, that the relationships between Jews and Christians have radically improved in these years. Where there was ignorance and therefore prejudice and stereotypes, there is now growing mutual knowledge, appreciation and respect. There is, above all, love between us; that kind of love, I mean, which is for both of us a fundamental injunction of our religious traditions, and which the New Testament has received from the Old. Love involves understanding. It also involves frankness and the freedom to disagree in a brotherly way where there are reasons for it.[1]

The Pope has repeatedly rejected any view that Judaism is somehow an incomplete religion or fossil of Christianity. For example, on November 26, 1986, in an address to the Jewish Community of Australia, the Pope urged that "Catholics should have not only respect but also great fraternal love, for it is the teaching of both the Hebrew and the Christian Scriptures that the Jews are beloved of God, who has called them with an irrevocable calling." The Pope had even recommended that the terms "Old Testament" and "New Testament" be replaced by the terms "Hebrew Bible" and "Christian Scriptures," though, of course, such old habits would be difficult to break.

Truly, the spirit of our age is in John Paul's blood. As a bishop he had been in Rome for all four conciliar sessions of Vatican II, where he defended the right of universal religious liberty and made vital contributions to *Lumen Gentium*. Because of this outstanding work, he was named a cardinal on July 9, 1967 by Paul VI, and ultimately, in 1978, became his successor.

The Pope's guidance figured prominently in the *Notes*. Indeed, he himself created the "remarkable formula," based on Paul's Epistle to the Romans, which summed up the Church's new theological outlook toward Judaism: The Jewish people were "the People of the Old Covenant that has never been revoked." Their existence, their covenant, was a living, permanent gift of God to the world.

The spirit of Vatican II could be felt even in his very first audience with Jewish representatives on March 12, 1979:

> It is useful to refer once more to the council declaration *Nostra Aetate* and to repeat what the *Guidelines* say about the repudiation of "all forms of anti-semitism and discrimination," as "opposed to the very spirit of Christianity," but "which in any case the dignity of the human person alone would suffice to condemn." The Catholic Church therefore clearly repudiates in principle, and in practice, all such violations of human rights wherever they may occur throughout the world.

Under his guidance, a Pontifical Commission in 1988 issued a brutal condemnation of the most vicious kind of anti-semitism the world has ever seen, Nazi anti-semitism:

> It is well known that the Nationalist-Socialist totalitarian party made a racist ideology the basis of its insane program, aimed at the physical elimination of those it deemed belonging to inferior races. This party became responsible for one of the greatest genocides in history. This murderous folly struck *first and foremost* the Jewish people in unheard-of proportions. [emphasis added]

And his commission also took aim at modern-day anti-semitism, whose anti-Zionism "serves at times as a screen for anti-semitism, feeding on it and leading to it." Condemnation was also made of those "countries [that] impose undue harassments and restrictions on the free emigration of Jews."

It is important to realize that the Pope's vehemence against anti-semitism is not just a result of his Vatican II roots, but also the result of his deep personal roots: A short distance from Wadowice, the small market town where the Pope was born, is *Auschwitz,* known as *Oswiecim* to Poles. For them, too, it is a place of horror; thousands upon thousands of Poles lost their lives there.

This Polish Pope knows the horrors of Nazism all too intimately. At the time he was growing up, many of the artists and philosophers in Crakow were Jewish. They befriended him. They taught him. And he suffered to see some of the most significant people in his life sent to extermination camps, together with hoards of his own Polish people. Therefore, to the Pope the terror of Nazism is something that Jews and Christians *share together,* as he expressed on June 7, 1979, in his homily at Auschwitz:

> I have come and I kneel on this Golgotha of the modern world, on these tombs, largely nameless like the great Tomb of the Unkown Soldier. I kneel before all the inscriptions that come one after another bearing the memory of the victims of Oswiecim in the languages: Polish, English, Bulgarian, Romany, Czech, Danish, French, Greek, Hebrew, Yiddish, Spanish, Flemish, Serbo-Croat, German, Norwegian, Russian, Romanian, Hungarian and Italian.

This is not to say that the Pope minimalizes the fate of Jews during the Holocaust, attempting to blur their suffering with that of others. Quite to the contrary, he has emphasized that the suffering of Jews is beyond comparison:

> In particular I pause with you, dear participants in this encounter, before the inscription in Hebrew. This inscription awakens the memory of the people whose sons and daugh-

ters were intended for total extermination. This people draws its origin from Abraham, our father in faith (cf. Rom 4:12), as was expressed by Paul of Tarsus. The very people who received from God the commandment "thou shalt not kill" itself experienced in a special measure what is meant by killing. It is not permissible for anyone to pass by this inscription with indifference.

For the Pope, the Nazi threat to destroy the Jews was also a threat to the very roots from which Christianity draws its strength. And as we all know, if the roots are severed, the plant dies. Therefore, to the Pope and the Church, anyone who violates the integrity and rights of the Jewish people, anyone that threatens the living biblical spirit of the Jewish people, violates the Christian faith. For this reason,

> If Christians must consider themselves brothers of all men and behave accordingly, this holy obligation is all the more binding when they find themselves before members of the Jewish people![2]

We are brothers and sisters. That is the message of John Paul II. That was the same message he proclaimed to the entire world on Sunday, April 13, 1986, when the Holy Father made history by visiting the synagogue in Rome — *the first visit to a synagogue by a pope in the history of the world.*[3] It is such a remarkable speech, that we have included its high-lights here as a model for Jewish-Catholic dialogue:

This gathering in a way brings to a close, after the Pontificate of John XXIII and the Second Vatican Council, a long period which we must not tire of reflecting upon in order to draw from it the appropriate lessons. Certainly, we cannot and should not forget that the historical circumstances of the past were very different from those that have laboriously matured over the centuries. The general acceptance of a legitimate plurality on the social, civil, and religious levels has been arrived at with great difficulty. Nevertheless, a consideration of centuries-long cultural conditioning could not prevent us from recognizing that the acts of discrimination, unjustified limitation of religious freedom, oppression also on the level of civil freedom in regard to the Jews were, from an objective point of view, gravely deplorable manifestations. Yes, once again, through myself, the Church, in the words of the well-known Declaration *Nostra Aetate* (no. 4), "deplored the hatred, persecutions, and displays of anti-semitism directed against the Jews at any time and by anyone"; I repeat: "by anyone" [i.e., including the Church].

I would like once more to express a word of abhorrence for the genocide decreed against the Jewish people during the last War, which led to the *holocaust* of millions of innocent victims.

When I visited on June 1979 the concentration camp at Auschwitz and prayed for the many victims from various nations, I paused in particular before the memorial stone with the inscription in Hebrew and thus manifested the sentiments of my heart: "This inscription stirs the memory of the People whose sons and daughters were destined to total extermination. This People has its origin in Abraham, who is our father in faith (cf. Rom 4:12), as Paul of Tarsus expressed it. Precisely this People, which received from God the commandment: 'Thou shalt not kill' has experienced in itself to a particular degree what killing means. Before this inscription it is not permissible for anyone to pass by with indifference. . . ."

The Jewish community of Rome too paid a high price in blood.

And it was surely a significant gesture that in those dark years of racial persecution the doors of our religious houses, of our churches, of the Roman Seminary, of buildings belonging to the Holy See and of Vatican City itself were thrown open to offer refuge and safety to so many Jews of Rome being hunted by their persecutors.

Today's visit is meant to make a decisive contribution to the consolidation of the good relations between our two communities, in imitation of the example of so many men and women who have worked and who are still working today, on both sides, to overcome old prejudices and secure ever wider and fuller recognition of that "bond" and that "common spiritual patrimony" that exists between Jews and Christians. . . .

The Jewish religion is not "extrinsic" to us, but in a certain way is "intrinsic" to our own religion. With Judaism therefore we have a relationship which we do not have with any other religion. You are our dearly beloved brothers and, in a certain way, it could be said that you are our elder brothers. . . .

No ancestral or collective blame can be imputed to the Jews as a people for "what happened in Christ's passion" (cf. *Nostra Aetate*). Not indiscriminately to the Jews of that time, nor to those who came afterward, nor to those of today. So any alleged theological justification for discriminatory measures or, worse still, for acts of persecution is unfounded. The Lord will judge each one "according to his own works," Jews and Christians alike (cf. Rom 2:6). . . .

It is not lawful to say that the Jews are "repudiated or cursed," as if this were taught or could be deduced from the sacred scriptures of the Old or the New Testament (cf. *Nostra Aetate*). Indeed, the Council had already said in this same text of *Nostra Aetate*, and also in the Dogmatic Constitution *Lumen Gentium*, no. 16, referring to Saint Paul in the Letter to the Romans (11:28-29), that the Jews are beloved of God, who has called them with an irrevocable calling.

On these convictions rest our present relations. On the occasion of this visit to your synagogue, I wish to reaffirm them and to proclaim them in their perennial value.

For this is the meaning which is to be attributed to my visit to you, to the Jews of Rome.

It was revolutionary. It was dramatic. It was an historic first. The Pope's visit to the synagogue in Rome proclaimed to the world that the spirit of our age was here. No longer were the ideas of Vatican II just the province of theologians and scholars. The Pope had brought them down to grass roots.

The effect cannot be overestimated. With the Pope's visit, Judaism was legitimized before the entire Christian world as a true world religion. The synagogue too was legitimized as a true house of God. After all, if the Pope could enter a synagogue without undermining his faith, other Catholics could certainly feel comfortable doing the same, following his example.

Judaism was indeed alive. It had not died with the advent of Christianity. Judaism was flourishing, still living proof of its irrevocable covenant. Judaism was the living "elder brother" of Christianity, to be loved *as a brother.* By opening his arms to Jews as "elder brothers," "dearly beloved brothers," the Pontiff personally proclaimed our "spiritual bond," the essence of *Nostra Aetate.* Moreover, he personally set an example by faithfully following the suggestions of the *Guidelines* and *Notes.*

This visit is even more dramatic when you consider the unfortunate sentiment that exists among many Jews that the Polish people are somehow more anti-semitic, or even innately anti-semitic. There are many reasons for this prejudice; and it *is* a prejudice. For one thing, most of the concentration camps were in Polish territories, and some Jews feel that this could not have occurred without Polish cooperation. For another thing, most of the Jewish survivors from World War II are Polish, and therefore their particular anguish is very prominent within world Jewish opinion. Nevertheless, if there has been anti-semitism on the part of Poles, there has also been "anti-polonism" on the part of Jews. We must remind ourselves that the vast majority of both peoples, however, have been God-fearing and free of this kind of malicious hatred.

From the Pope's perspective, Jews and Poles are in a way very similar. Both peoples, both nations, have experienced extreme oppression at the hands of others. The Polish people have for centuries been undermined, abused, persecuted, and enslaved by many nations. Just as in the case of Jews, there is a huge Polish *Diaspora,* a dispersion of Polish refugees throughout the world in the United States, Great Britain, Canada, France and Australia.

Indeed, the Nazis hated the Poles almost as much as the Jews. If the Jews were chosen as the Nazi's first victims, it is clear from many of Hitler's statements that he intended the Poles to be next. Until he could exterminate them, however, he considered them to be "useful" as slave laborers. And we must remind ourselves that the overwhelming majority of the Polish people are Catholic. Therefore, the Pope is adamant that Catholics never forget the destructiveness of Nazism, and that, as an act of faith, they guard against it happening again in the future.

In this, Jews and Catholics must stand together, just as Pope John Paul II stood together with the Chief Rabbi Elio Toaf in the synagogue in Rome.

On that momentous day, John Paul II, true to the biblical story of Jacob and Esau, showed that the "younger brother" could indeed embrace the "elder brother." Christianity could indeed embrace Judaism.

"Brothers." A simple word, yet it says far more than all the words in the previous three documents combined.

Forgiveness

With the historic visit of the Pope to the synagogue in Rome, the reconciliation between Jews and Catholics had gone from the impersonal to the personal, from words on paper to words between people. There was a new history between us fully alive in the present. Unfortunately, alive too, was the memory of a painful past.

But the past is not just something you should ever toss away and forget. Quite to the contrary, it must be remembered, heeded, learned from, so that it will never repeat itself. Only by remembering the mistakes of the past and by setting up the proper safeguards against them, can we prevent these from recurring in the present.

On the other hand, no one should be so obsessed with the past, that they prevent themselves from moving into the future. No one should *live* in the past. No one can guide themselves forward, if they are constantly looking backward.

How does one recognize the past, but not be bound to it? How does one rise above history, without erasing it? For religious people, Jews and Christians alike, the answer is the foundation of both of our faiths: *repentance* and *forgiveness*.

In 1990, a meeting was scheduled of the International Catholic-Jewish Liaison Committee. The agenda for this meeting was to be a discussion of the history of anti-semitism within Christian countries. The site of this meeting was to be Prague, Czechoslovakia, and the choice turned out to be significant.

Due to the tremendous economic and social upheaval following the collapse of the Soviet Union, with the all-too-human tendency to seek "scapegoats," there was a large-scale resurgence of anti-semitism within Russia and Eastern Europe. Naturally, Jewish leaders were alarmed, and many requested that the proposed meeting not only discuss anti-semitism in the past, but the new wave of anti-semitism in the present. The Church, equally concerned about the problem, agreed wholeheartedly.

Yet, the world Jewish community was totally unprepared for what was to take place. Unbeknownst to them, the Church, true to her own conscience, teachings, and humanity, and true to the spirit of our age, in a declaration fully authorized and approved by the Holy Father himself, had decided to greet her Jewish brothers and sisters with another historic first: *the public repentance by the Church of her past sins of anti-semitism, and the request for forgiveness from the Jews for any wrongs perpetrated on them:*

That anti-semitism has found a place in Christian thought and practice calls for an act of *Teshuvah* and of reconciliation on our part, as we gather here in this city, which is a witness to our failure to be authentic witnesses to our faith at times in the past.

This was just part of then Archbishop, now Cardinal, Edward Idris Cassidy's opening remarks to the meeting; its timing couldn't have been more appropriate. How could the Church effectively deal with the problem of modern-day anti-semitism without first dealing with ancient anti-semitism? How could Catholics and the Jews work together to fight this scourge, unless the Church did something to heal the lingering resentment among the Jewish people for the past? We both had to move forward without looking back, yet acknowledge where we had come from.

The reaction from the world Jewish community was phenomenal. Many felt that a new honesty had been reached, that members of the Church could only now truly be considered "brothers and sisters" in the spiritual sense of that word. In using the Hebrew word, "Teshuvah," which signifies a "turning away" from past wrong-doing, yet simultaneously a "returning to" a righteous relationship with both man and God, a new plateau in our relationship was reached. If *Nostra Aetate* was the seed of our age, this was the fruit.

Needless to say, such a statement could not help but get the meeting off on a good note. Cassidy's opening remarks also addressed the pain and suffering experienced by Jews under the Nazis. In addition, he highlighted the theological implications of Nazism — it was, in its very essence, a turning away from human conscience and morality, from the very purpose of the covenant, whether "old" or "new." Quoting a Jewish teacher, Rabbi Abraham Joshua Heschel, he remarked:

Nazism in its very roots was a rebellion against the Bible, against the God of Abraham. Realizing that it was Christianity that implanted attachment to the God of Abraham and involvement with the Hebrew Bible in the hearts of Western man, Nazism resolved that it must both exterminate the Jews and eliminate Christianity, and bring about instead a revival of Teutonic paganism. Nazism has suffered a defeat, but the process of eliminating the Bible from the consciousness of the Western world goes on. It is on the issue of saving the radiance of the Hebrew Bible in the minds of man that Jews and Christians are called upon to work together. None of us can do it alone. *Both of us must realize that in our age anti-semitism is anti-Christianity and that anti-Christianity is anti-semitism.* [emphasis added]

Cassidy continued, urging Christians "to take the initiative" to help eliminate all forms of anti-semitism: "If we are to serve him [God] we must also love each and every one of those whom he has created; and we do that by showing respect and concern for our neighbor, by promoting peace and justice, by knowing how to pardon."

In regard to the new wave of anti-semitism in Eastern Europe, Cassidy's statement was taken quite seriously indeed. The Church, working together with the world Jewish community as brothers and sisters, issued what is now called the "Prague Statement."[1] It outlined a series of six steps to help contain the new epidemic:

1. Translation of all the new Church documents dealing with Jews and Judaism.

2. Including these teachings in theological seminaries.

3. Monitoring all the events regarding an upsurge of anti-semitism, with an eye to counter them.

4. Continued actions to support freedom of worship and religious education for all citizens regardless of faith.

5. Support of general legislation aimed at eliminating discrimination on the grounds of race or religion, or incitement to religious or racial hatred; this would include curtailing the freedom of racist organizations to congregate.

6. General education measures which teach respect for different civilizations, cultures and religions, with the elimination of all racially- or religiously-prejudiced textbooks.

The historic meeting in Prague can be summed up best by the final three paragraphs of the statement:

After two millennia of estrangement and hostility, we have a sacred duty as Catholics and Jews to strive to create a genuine culture of mutual esteem and reciprocal caring.

Catholic-Jewish dialogue can become a sign of hope and inspiration to other religions, races, and ethnic groups to turn away from contempt, toward realizing authentic human fraternity.

This new spirit of friendship and caring for one another may be the most important symbol we have to offer to our troubled world.

The first real-life test of the Prague Statement would not take place in Czechoslovakia, but in Poland instead. Poland too had been devastated by economic and social upheaval. Poland too had been experiencing waves of anti-semitic scapegoating. Moreover, as mentioned earlier, Poland had the unfortunate reputation among Jews as somehow being more anti-semitic than other nations. It was the sincere desire on the part of Pope John Paul II that this reputation of Poland be cleansed, and that his very own nation become the nucleus for "this new spirit of friendship and caring," which needed to spread throughout Central Europe.

How to achieve such an ambitious goal? The vehicle chosen by the Pope stands out as one of the most tremendous achievements of our age. On January 20, 1991, a statement was prepared by the Polish Church, and read out loud "without comment and with the full authority of the Polish bishops," simultaneously to every Polish person in the more than six thousand parishes throughout Poland. This "Polish

Bishop's Statement," as it is now known, called upon the entire Polish Catholic community.

The "Polish Bishop's Statement" emphasized the close spiritual bond between the Catholic Church and the Jewish People: "There is no other religion with which the Church has such close relations, nor is there any other people with which it is so closely linked." This closeness was declared by Pope John Paul II personally, when he entered the synagogue in Rome and referred to Jews as "our elder brothers" in the faith.

"The Church, as God's people of the new election and covenant, did not disinherit God's people of the first election and covenant of the gifts received by God." Jews were still well-loved by God, and therefore any anti-semitism was a sin against God. Jews today could not be held responsible for the death of Jesus.

However the statement went well beyond a mere repetition and reinforcement of previous Church documents. It emphasized the strong historical ties between the Jews and the Polish people, ties that began as early as the first centuries of Polish history. Drawing heavily on the speeches of John Paul II, the "Polish Bishop's Statement" addressed the suffering of the Polish Jews during the Holocaust. Polish Catholic suffering simply "did not reach the same extent; there was not time for it to reach the same extent." Therefore, in a way, Polish Jews bore the "awful sacrifice of destruction" for all of Poland. For this, they must be honored.

Many Poles saved Jews during the last war. Hundreds, if not thousands, paid for this with their own lives and the lives of their loved ones. . . .

In spite of so many heroic examples on the part of Polish Christians, there were also people who remained indifferent to this incomprehensible tragedy. We are especially disheartened by those among the Catholics who in some way were the cause of the death of Jews. *They will forever gnaw at our conscience on the social plane. If only one Christian could have helped and did not stretch out a helping hand to a Jew during the time of danger or caused his death, we must ask for forgiveness of our Jewish brothers and sisters. . . . We express our sincere regret for all the incidents of anti-semitism which were committed at any time or by anyone on Polish soil.* [emphasis added]

This is just a brief summary of some of the highlights of the "Polish Bishop's Statement." However, its significance cannot be emphasized enough. If many Jews had once criticized the Catholic Church for not appearing to act more decisively when anti-semitism arose in pre-Nazi Germany, it is clear that history's lesson had been well-learned. With the "Prague Statement" and the subsequent "Polish Bishop's Statement," the Church has taken bold, decisive actions to quell the kind of anti-semitism and political scapegoating which had engulfed the earth in the Holocaust a generation earlier.

Just imagine what history might be like had both Jews and Catholics worked together this way when Nazism had reared its ugly head in Germany. We cannot go backward and fix our mistakes. However, if we do not forget our mistakes and learn from them, they can become the lessons upon which a saner future can be built. All we have to do is recognize our errors, repent of them, ask forgiveness from those we have wronged, and show our firmest commitment to not repeat them again. This is exactly what the Catholic Church has done.

This feat is something which must be respected, if not applauded, by Jews around the world. Forgiveness and repentance are the very cornerstone of the Jewish religion. The Church has formally repented of her sins and requested forgiveness from her Jewish "elder brothers." Should Jews not forgive her?

This is not at all an easy task for many Jews. Many Jews continue to be suspicious and question how long our age will really last. This is understandable considering the many centuries of mistrust between us.

Nevertheless, as Jews, as a people of God, Jews must forgive. Jewish law considers it "cruel" not to forgive after someone has made a sincere repentance.[2] Jewish teaching considers it wrong to "bear a grudge" against someone who has offered a sincere apology and shown their commitment not to repeat the sins of the past.[3] And even if it is impossible to forgive completely yet, Jews should make every attempt to work toward that goal.

Forgiveness is a process. Once the process is begun, if every person works at it, forgiveness can grow stronger and stronger every day. It is a process that Jews and Catholics can undertake together, each one encouraging the other to let go of more prejudice, more pain, more anger, more grudges — until with every breath, Jews and Catholic infuse the new spirit of our age into the world.

"Forgive us." "We forgive." No words more powerful have ever been spoken.

Israel and the Church

When *Nostra Aetate* first declared the spiritual link between Jews and Catholics, who could have imagined all the events that have taken place? Who would have imagined an authentic friendship to emerge after centuries of mistrust? Who would have expected the Pope to actually enter a synagogue? Who would have predicted profound repentance of anti-semitism and a massive campaign against a major anti-semitic upsurge?

And yet, even more miracles were to take place. On December 30, 1993, corresponding to the sixteenth day of the month of Tevet in the year 5754 of the Jewish calendar, the Holy See established full diplomatic relations with the modern State of Israel.

Next to the giving of the Torah at Sinai, the resurrection of Israel is for Jews perhaps the single most important event in the history of Judaism. It restored the hopes and dreams of a dispersed people — a people despised, rejected, and killed, simply because, as the Pope stated in his homily at Auschwitz, they were Jewish. The birth of the modern State of Israel is for Jews a concrete sign of the continued vitality and creativity of the Jewish people.

Therefore, when the Holy See established full diplomatic relations with the State of Israel, it was far more than a mere brotherly gesture. For Jews, it was a powerful symbol of full recognition and legitimacy, an open declaration to the world that Judaism continues to have a purpose in God's plan for human history. It was a sign that Jews were truly loved by their Catholic brothers and sisters and welcome in the family of nations. The fifteen-point agreement would have the force of a treaty under international law.

What was responsible for this stunning diplomatic achievement? The spirit of our age. The Preamble to the agreement echoed many of the words we have already seen:

> The Holy See and the State of Israel, mindful of the singular character and universal significance of the Holy Land; aware of the unique nature of the relationship between the Catholic Church and the Jewish people, of the historic process of reconciliation and growth in mutual understanding and friendship between Catholics and Jews . . . agreed upon the following articles. . .

Yet, as extraordinary as this event was, many Jews felt a tremendous sadness, if not anger. Many felt that this step had taken far too long; that after decades of trying to pick up the pieces from the Holocaust, the recognition of Israel by the Church should have taken place much sooner.

The fact is though, such recognition *did* take place considerably sooner. Israel had already been recognized by the Holy See for quite some time. Certain diplomatic relations had always existed between the Church and Israel; the Israeli Embassy in Rome had an officer that communicated to the Vatican Secretariat of State; the Apostolic Delegation in Jerusalem communicated to the Israeli Ministry of Foreign Affairs.

Pope John Paul II had repeatedly recognized the State of Israel in many addresses:

The Hebrew people after tragic experiences, after suffering the extermination of so many sons and daughters, willing for security, has given life to the State of Israel.[1]

For the Hebrew people, living in the State of Israel and having for that land a precious testimony of faith, we want security and just tranquility and peace, that are basic for any nation and a condition of life and progress for any society.[2]

After the tragic extermination of the *Shoah,* the Hebrew People has started a new period of its history. Like any civil nation, it has a right to a country, in accordance with international law.[3]

I express particularly my solidarity with everyone in the State of Israel who is suffering for the deprecable bombardments.[4]

The Church has repeatedly recognized the State of Israel. The Israeli delegation was among the official delegations sent to the funeral of Pope Pius XII, the opening and closing of Vatican II, the funeral of John XXIII, and the inauguration of John Paul II. Paul VI made an official visit to Israel in January of 1964, and many Israeli leaders returned the visit over the years.[5]

The December 1993 agreement is not therefore *recognition per se* for Israel. The agreement *formalizes* relations between the Holy See and Israel. Now there is a full exchange of ambassadors, residing in established embassies within Israel and Rome. The relationship has now a true sense of permanence and international respect, which was not present before.

If it seemed that the Church was slow to give such an honor to Israel, this is simply not the case. Other countries such as South Africa, the Kingdom of Jordan, Saudia Arabia, Mexico, and the previous Soviet Union also waited a considerable length of time. And remarkably, full diplomatic relations with the United States were only formalized in 1984!

This is not to say that the relationship between the Church and Israel is not complicated. It is not a coincidence that the agreement occurred soon after the Gulf War, when the international climate toward Israel was most favorable, and when resistance to the accord would have been minimal. Such caution on the part of the Church is warranted. The Church is in a most delicate position, and Jews should reflect upon this more carefully. Because of her spiritual bond to Jews, the Church must appreciate the importance of this ancient biblical land, since it is at the very basis of the covenant she herself shares. Yet, because of her commitment to universal peace and prosperity, she cannot ignore concerns of the Arab peoples either, no less God's children. And because there are so many Catholic faithful residing within both Israel and other Middle Eastern nations, she must also be careful to protect and safeguard her flock — not an easy task in a war-torn area which has been subject to numerous terrorist attacks. Indeed, in any matter concerning Israel, the Church has to be concerned with far more than Israel.

Therefore, it is unfair for some Jews to expect the Church to give blanket support to Israel and every Israeli policy as a sign of firm Catholic commitment to the Jewish people. It is equally unfair to consider every disagreement between the Church and the policies of Israel as backsliding into a now repented anti-semitic past. Quite to the contrary, when you consider the difficult political aura around Israel, the worrisome violence in the area, the fear of retaliation by terrorists, the Church has been *amazingly forthright* in her support of Israel.

This support for Israel stems from the common history and spiritual brotherhood of Jews and Catholics. It is important to understand, however, that it is not based on any particular theological interpretation of the meaning of Israel, as the *Notes* makes clear:

> The existence of the State of Israel and its political options should be envisaged not in a

perspective which is in itself religious, but in their reference to the common principles of international law.

Some Jews misinterpret this as meaning that the Church *denies* that Israel is a "*Jewish* state," or that the Church *denies* that modern Israel is the continuation of God's promise to Abraham. This, however, is not the case. The Church would never deny that God keeps his promise and continues to love and help the Jewish people.

However, since no one can know God's will completely, the Church is cautious in drawing theological conclusions from contemporary political events. For one thing, any interpretation the Church might give would necessarily be Christian; after all, the Church has her own understanding of the Hebrew Bible and of the meaning of God's actions through history. Therefore, out of respect for the beliefs of her "elder brothers," the Church very carefully does not offer such religious interpretation.

For another thing, there is also the problem of militant fundamentalism, which is of great concern to the Church. Some fundamentalist Muslims desire Israel's destruction. Some fundamentalist Jews wish to banish Muslims from Israel and even to blow up the Dome of the Rock, the Islamic holy site which sits on the site of the Temple of Solomon. And, of course, some fundamentalist Christians see war in the Middle East as being the "armageddon" necessary for Jesus' return. Such dangerous mixtures of religion and politics is something the Church wishes to avoid.

Therefore, the establishment of full diplomatic relations, based on humanitarian principles of international law, is a true act of wisdom on the part of the Church. These principles are beyond divisive theological debates, and they cannot be distorted by particular religious groups with separate agendas. They are firmly established and universally accepted.

These principles are reflected in the entire agreement. From the very onset, both the State of Israel and the Holy See affirm the right of all human beings to "freedom of religion and conscience." Both "are committed to appropriate cooperation in fighting all forms of anti-semitism, racism, and religious intolerance, and in promoting mutual understanding among nations, tolerance among communities, and respect for human life and dignity."

Specifically, "The Holy See" reiterates "its condemnation of hatred, persecution and all other manifestations of anti-semitism directed against the Jewish people and individual Jews anywhere, at any time, and by anyone. In particular, the Holy See deplores attacks on Jews and desecration of Jewish synagogues and cemeteries, acts which offend the memory of the victims of the Holocaust, especially when they occur in the same place which witnessed it."

At the same time, the State of Israel agreed to "continuing respect for and protection of the character proper to Catholic sacred places, such as churches, monasteries, convents, cemeteries and their like," as well as "the continuing guarantee of the freedom of

Catholic worship." The Catholic Church has the right to maintain its own media communications, its own institutions and educational facilities, provided they do so in harmony with Israeli law.

Both the Holy See and the State of Israel have agreed to promote and encourage "cultural exchanges between Catholic institutions worldwide and educational, cultural and research institutions in Israel." Access to "manuscripts, historical documents and similar source materials" has been guaranteed, provided it is "in conformity with applicable laws and regulations."

Most importantly, in regard to the difficult conflict surrounding the State of Israel and her neighbors, the Holy See is committed to remaining neutral in this conflict:

> The Holy See, while maintaining in every case the right to exercise its moral and spiritual teaching office, deems it opportune to recall that, owing to its own character, it is solemnly committed to remaining neutral to all merely temporal conflicts, specifically to disputed territories and unsettled borders.

With the historic accord between Israel and the Holy See, the spirit of our age was now fully alive on the international level.

All the mutual respect, all the deep abiding spiritual connection between Jews and Catholics, were now infused into the political reality of the world.

Educating a New Generation

How do we energize the process of forgiveness and reconciliation, and guarantee a new future? How do we institutionalize a new spirit of friendship between Jews and Catholics? There is no more effective way than education.

Without proper education, the spirit of our age cannot fully spread its wings. Without proper education, people remain locked in their old ways, entrenched in bitter memories and fears. *Nostra Aetate* in essence marked a revolution in education, the beginning of a new Church teaching on Jews and Judaism. This teaching needs to be brought back home to individual people and, most importantly, to our children, upon whom our future depends. This teaching needs to become part of the fabric of Catholic home life, part of the spiritual education of every living Catholic child around the world.

In January 25, 1985, Pope John Paul II convoked a Synod of Bishops in order to honor the twentieth anniversary of the close of Vatican II. It was here that the Synod Fathers requested the Pope to authorize the creation of a new "catechism or compendium of all Catholic doctrine regarding both faith and morals." This would serve as a model upon which all local catechisms around the world would be based. All the new teachings of Vatican II, including the revolutionary new teachings about Jews and Judaism, were to be included.

The request bore fruit on June 25, 1992, when the Holy Father approved the new *Catechism of the Catholic Church*, the result of "six years of intense work done in a spirit of complete openness and fervent zeal," as the Pope described it.

In terms of the relationship between Jews and Catholics, the new world catechism is a breakthrough. It completely eradicates the foundation for the "teaching of contempt," which was summed up by Jules Isaac in three points:

1. The teaching that Jews were to be blamed for the death of Christ.

2. The lack of recognition for the Jewish contribution to Christianity.

3. The lack of recognition and respect for the spiritual teachings of rabbinic Judaism.

In the new catechism we cannot find any one of these. Indeed, the "teaching of contempt" has been completely transformed into the "teaching of respect."

This catechism is "state of the art." It contains in distilled form the entire new teaching on Jews and Judaism. And the new catechism is *doctrine*. Many of the doctrinal statements of Vatican II will never be read by the average citizen. Yet, through the catechism they shall be read, studied, *and lived* by millions of Catholics around the world.

Moreover, this new teaching on Jews and Judaism is communicated with a tone of warmth, love, and respect for the Church's "elder brothers," conveying that very same feeling that Pope John Paul II brought to the synagogue in Rome.

Therefore, in a way, the new catechism can serve as a kind of synthesis of the events, the documents, and the teachings of our age, both in thought and feeling. All the doors that have been opened since our age began are there for all to walk through. And, by way of a summary, we highlight them here:

Universal Salvation is possible for all God's children.

The new catechism teaches that all peoples of the world are blessed with the possibility of redemption by God, Christian and non-Christian alike. Quoting *Lumen Gentium* 16, it affirms:

"Those who, through no fault of their own, do not know the gospel of Christ or his Church, but who nevertheless seek God with a sincere heart and, moved by grace, try in their actions to do his will as they know it through the dictates of their conscience, those too may achieve eternal salvation" (# 847).

There is an eternal, irrevocable covenant between God and the Jewish people.

The new catechism teaches that the Jewish people should be accorded eternal respect, due to their unique and special relationship with God. The "New"

Covenant did not eradicate the "Old." The "Old" or Original Covenant is the eternally-active gift of God to the Jewish People, the foundation upon which the Christian calling is built (# 839).

The Jewish people were "the first to hear the Word of God. . . . To the Jews belong 'the sonship, the glory, the covenants, the giving of the law, the worship and the promise; to them belong the patriarchs, and of their race, according to the flesh, is the Christ' (Rom 9:4-5), 'for the gifts and the call of God are irrevocable' (Rom 11:29)."

Both Jews and Catholics are linked together in awaiting the culmination of God's kingdom.

The new catechism emphasizes the eternal relationship between Jews and Christians, and their mutual participation in helping to bring about the salvation of the world: "And when one considers the future, God's People of the Old Covenant and the new People of God tend toward similar goals: expectation of the coming (or the return) of the Messiah" (# 840).

Jews and Catholics may still differ in certain theological viewpoints, but we both await the coming of the Messianic age, when both our views shall be reconciled by God.

The Jewish people as a group are not responsible for Jesus' death.

A testimony to the work of Jules Isaac and Pope John XXIII, the new catechism states:

"[N]either all Jews indiscriminately at that time, nor Jews today, can be charged with the crimes committed during his Passion. . . . [T]he Jews should not be spoken of as rejected or accursed as if this followed from holy scripture.

"*The personal sin of the participants (Judas, the Sanhedrin, Pilate) is known to God alone.* Hence we cannot lay responsibility for the trial on the Jews in Jerusalem as a whole, despite the outcry of a *manipulated* crowd" (# 597). [emphasis added]

Jesus had a close relationship with the Jewish sages, the Pharisees, sharing many of their beliefs.

The new catechism teaches that Jesus often praised the Pharisees (Mk 12:34, Lk 7:36; 14:1). Resurrection of the dead, almsgiving, fasting and prayer, the custom of addressing God as Father, and the commandment to love God and neighbor are all teachings Jesus shared with these noble Jewish sages (# 575).

Only "*certain* Pharisees and partisans of Herod, together with priests and scribes [i.e., not *all* priests and scribes]" had banned together to betray Jesus (# 574). [emphasis added]

The Romans, Gentile pagans, were largely responsible for Jesus' death.

The new catechism teaches that the Jewish court system at the time of Jesus was not responsible for condemning him to death. This was the work of Imperial Rome.

Only certain Jews, who were collaborators with pagan Rome, participated in handing Jesus over "to the Gentiles to be mocked and scourged and crucified (Mk 8:31; Mt 20:19)." The "sanhedrin [the Jewish court[1]] . . . having lost the right to put anyone to death, han[ded] him over to the Romans" (#'s 596, 572).

The devout Jew he was,
Jesus upheld and practiced Jewish law.

The new catechism teaches that Jesus did not come to abolish Jewish law (Mt 5:17-19). Moreover, Jesus himself kept Jewish law "in its all-embracing detail — according to his own words, down to 'the least of these commandments' (Mt 5:19)" (#'s 577, 578, 579).

Jesus had the utmost respect and love
for the Temple in Jerusalem.

Jesus "like the prophets before him," had only "the deepest respect for the Temple" (#583). Section 584 states that "Jesus went up to the Temple as the privileged place of encounter with God." It was this love of God's Temple that motivated him to drive out the money-lenders and not his rebellion against the institutions of Judaism in general. Jesus even paid the "temple tax" (#586). This reverence for the Temple was continued by Jesus' apostles even after his resurrection.

87

Therefore, any across-the-board notion that somehow the Temple in Jerusalem was so corrupt that Jesus came to destroy it, is simply not true. Christians should honor the great Temple of Jerusalem in their memory, just as Jews do.

Jewish liturgy is the foundation of Christian liturgy, and should be respected and studied.

"A better knowledge of the Jewish people's faith and religious life as professed and lived even now can help our better understanding of certain aspects of Christian liturgy. For both Jews and Christians sacred scripture is an essential part of their respective liturgies: in the proclamation of the Word of God, the response to this word, prayer of praise and intercession for the living and the dead, invocation of God's mercy. In its characteristic structure, the liturgy of the Word originates in Jewish prayer" (# 1096).

Therefore, Christians should have only the utmost respect for Judaism as it is practiced today. After all, Christian worship truly draws its strength from these very same Jewish roots.

Last but certainly not least:

Prejudice against Jews or against any other people is a sin.

Infused with the great humanitarianism of Pope John XXIII, the new catechism teaches that "the equality of men rests essentially on their dignity as persons and the rights that flow from it. Every form of social or cultural discrimination in fundamental personal rights on the grounds of sex, race, color, social conditions, language, or religion must be curbed and eradicated as incompatible with God's design" (# 1935).

Therefore, Christians today must actively seek to abolish all discrimination and prejudice, in their actions and in their thoughts. And since anti-semitism *is* discrimination, Catholics have a religious obligation to work to eliminate it from their thoughts, from their actions, and from all aspects of society.

Truly, the new catechism *is* "state of the art"; the "teaching of respect."

With it, the light of our age will be able to shine on child after child, in city after city, nation after nation. Loving words of respect for Jews and Judaism will ring out in all the earth's languages, heard in Catholic classrooms and homes around the world.

The new catechism is a new teaching for a new generation. A new generation of Catholic and Jewish children who, for the first time in history, have an opportunity to grow up without prejudice, and help create a new world.

Conclusion:
Creating a New World

So here we are. Jews. Christians. Each with *separate* understandings of God's plan for human history, and each with *shared* understandings of God's plan for human history. And yet, both part of the one history of humankind proclaimed by Genesis.

Where do we go from here? If we can truly overcome the past, there is no limit to where we can go.

The religious divisiveness of the past centuries has created a good deal of mistrust for the values of religion. In the general population, religion is often seen as a force for creating separateness, polarization, and bigotry, rather than a force for creating unity, harmony and respect.

These days the truth of science is far more respected than the truth of religion. The structure of the atom is deemed more important than the "structure" of the human soul. The very existence of a human soul is doubted. The realm of the spirit has been taken over by psychiatrists, psychologists and sociologists.

Therefore, the vision of our age is far greater than the healing of the rift between Jews and Catholics. It is the vision of creating a new appreciation for God and religion in the world.

Our age is the beginning of a new age for religious values, where the theological differences between faiths are respected by all, but do not prevent religions from working together.

This is far more than the "ecumenism" of the recent past. Though Jews and Christians do work together on social matters, on legislative concerns, on charitable causes, on humanistic issues — this work has been weakened because we have been unable to feel comfortable with the fundamental theological differences that have separated us, or because we have still been entrenched in past pain.

Jews have often been reserved, somewhat afraid of "letting go" when cooperating with Christians, concerned that their full participation with the Church might be interpreted as their "endorsement" of Christian beliefs. Christians have welcomed Jews, but all too often they "walk on eggshells" to avoid any offense, even to the point of not expressing their own beliefs. In essence, what we have seen in the modern inter-religious movement, despite all its accomplishments, is Jews not being Jews, and Christians not being Christians. Each being unable to profess their deepest, most intimate religious beliefs in front of the other, afraid of undermining the other. Each all too guarded.

The promise of our age brings a fresh breeze.

With the repentance of the Church of her past anti-semitism, with her affirmation of the irrevocability of the Jewish people, and with her diplomatic support for the State of Israel, an opportunity to let go of the fear has finally come. Now, both Jews and Christians have an opportunity to be themselves. Jew.

Christian. Both affirming their own visions of God's truth; yet each capable of expressing that truth to the other, without divisiveness, without polarization. Each being able to engage in even the most intimate dialogue about faith and theological differences, without blurring the differences between us.

Jews and Christians are called by both their faiths to help redeem the world. This is the foundation of the Christian witness to Christ. This is expressed in the Jewish concept of *tikkun olam,* in which all Jews have a responsibility to *repair* the world.

In our age we can both affirm this call to action with a true, deeply felt, religious spirit. In our age we can bring new religious power to all inter-religious efforts, and therefore we have a real opportunity to create a new world.

Imagine if the spirit of reconciliation could begin first between Jews and Catholics, and then spread to include other Christians, Moslems, Hindus, all God's peoples, all those who seek truth with reverence for the Divine Mystery in their hearts? Imagine an epidemic of the deep understanding and "mutual respect" called for *Nostra Aetate* spreading around the world?

Our age is the nucleus of a new beginning, and yet an old beginning, for that was the very promise of the covenant of the Hebrew Bible. That was the very promise that God made to Abraham.

Both of us, Jews and Christians, consider ourselves "children of Abraham." Both feel called to bear witness to the One God, Creator and Redeemer. Both feel called to "walk before God" as a representative of righteousness in the world. Both of us feel called to work hard to eradicate "paganism" in the world, a world in which people worship money, political power, war, and all multiple man-made idols of society. In this sense, we are truly "brothers-in-faith," sharing in the promise that God made to all humankind through Abraham.

Can't we embrace this ancient promise with the new spirit of our age? Can't we both, as Jews and as Christians, work together to redeem the one world we both share?

It cannot happen unless the spirit of our age becomes the personal spirit of every Jew and Christian throughout the world.

If there is one Jew left in the world who still harbors a fear or grudge against a Christian for the past, if there is one Christian left in the world who still believes forcible baptism is the route to world salvation, then the promise of our age remains unfulfilled.

All Jews and Catholics must work on themselves as individual people to free their minds from the divisiveness of the past, and embrace this declaration for the future.

Certainly, this is not an easy process for anyone, for we are talking about human emotion: loves, hatreds, fears, angers, anguish. These must be delicately unravelled like fine threads.

Yet, the process can begin. Now. In our age. It is an age we both share, for it was founded by the spirit of Professor Jules Isaac and Pope John XXIII.

Shall we not bear witness to these extraordinary men, one Jewish, one Catholic? Shall we not add all our Jewish and Catholic voices to this song of forgiveness? Shall we not be joined in this by Protestants, Moslems, Hindus and Buddhists? Shall we not allow this song to ring out through every nation of the world, until all God's children are free from religious prejudice, until all can turn their eyes toward the One God who created us all?

This is what our age is all about. It is up to us, to make it real. It is up to us to create a new world together.

Notes

Introduction

1. Some of the Church's changes regarding Jews and Judaism had already begun to appear within certain Protestant denominations prior to 1965, notably the removal of blame from the entire Jewish people for the death of Jesus. However, because these went hand-in-hand with rigorous calls for conversion, Jews could hardly find them significant. See "Conclusion: Creating a New World," footnote #1.

Opening Doors

1. Gerhard M. Reigner, "*Nostra Aetate*: Twenty Years After," in *Fifteen Years of Catholic-Jewish Dialogue, 1970-1985* (Libreria Editrice Vaticana, 1988), p. 276. Hereafter cited as *Dialogue*.

2. Eugene Fischer, "The Evolution of a Tradition: From *Nostra Aetate* to the *Notes*," in *Dialogue*, p. 241.

3. That *Nostra Aetate*'s deploring of anti-semitism by anyone also included anti-semitism by the Church, was specifically stated by Pope John Paul II in his historic visit to the Rome synagogue, which we shall discuss later.

The Dialogue Begins

1. The term "old," as in Old Testament or Old Covenant, shall be placed in quotations to remind the reader that this does not imply that Judaism is either outdated or antiquated. This topic will be discussed in the next section.

2. As we shall discuss in the chapter "Elder Brothers," Pope John Paul II urged in his trip to Australia that the term "Hebrew Bible" be used instead of "Old Testament." It is a welcomed suggestion which many have already begun to follow. The authors would also like to suggest "Original Testament" as a suitable alternative.

3. In this regard, Rabbis Jack Bemporad and Joseph Ehrenkranz, together with Dr. Anthony Cenera, founded the CCJU, the Center for Christian-Jewish Undersanding, which is at Sacred Heart University, in Fairfield County, Connecticut.

Deepening the Understanding

1. Pope John Paul II in his address to the Jewish community of Mainz, Germany, November 17, 1980.

Elder Brothers

1. Pope John Paul II in his address to the American Jewish Committee, 1987.

2. Pope John Paul II in his address to the Jewish Community of Mainz, Germany, November 17, 1980.

3. Since Peter was the first Pope, and he was born Jewish, he is often considered the first Pope to enter a synagogue. However, such a visit is radically different from that of Pope John Paul II, after an 1800-year rent between Jews and Catholics.

Forgiveness

1. Rabbi Jack Bemporad was privileged to have gone to Rome on behalf of the International Jewish Committee on Interreligious Consultations (IJCIC), to negotiate the agenda of the Prague meeting. He led the Synagogue Council of America delegation to Prague and wrote the first draft of the Prague agreement. Cardinal Willebrands, Cardinal Cassidy's predecessor, incorporated it as an appendix to his own important work called, *Christian Jewish Dialogue.*

2. Moises Maimonides, *Mishneh Torah,* transl. Philip Birnbaum (New York: Hebrew Publishing Company, 1967), "Repentance," chap. 2, sect. 1, p. 36.

3. Ibid., sect. 10, p. 37.

Israel and the Church

1. Homily at Toronto, October 5, 1980.

2. Apostolic letter *Redemptionis Anno,* April 20, 1984.

3. Pope John Paul II in his speech to the leaders of the Jewish community in Miami, September 11, 1987.

4. General Audience, January 23, 1991.

5. Memorandum by Rabbi Leon Klenicki, February 4, 1991, to the IJCIC.

Educating A New Generation

1. According to Jewish scholars there is considerable evidence that the governing religious body at the time of Jesus was not the so-called "sanhedrin" but the "Bet Din," or *Boule* in Greek. The sanhedrin was a priestly tribunal, which, under the state of military occupation by the Romans, was used as a "puppet" to govern Judea. See, for example, Ellis Rivkin, "Beth Din, Boule, Sanhedrin: A Tragedy of Errors," Hebrew Union College Annual, vol. XLVI, 1975.

Conclusion: Creating a New World

1. Recent Protestant statements of the World Council of Churches 1988, the Lutheran Church 1994 and the Methodists 1996, are fully in the spirit of our age.